Dear Bride

Advice for the Newlywed

Written by Judy Smith

Design by Magdalena Snowman

Dear Bride,

Right now you are young and naive enough to believe in white lace and promises. That's OK, hold on to that feeling—you're about to enter into the ride of your life. It won't always be champagne toasts and gooey speeches with proclamations of love. A rough road lies ahead as you pull away amidst the view of "Just Married" in your starry eyes. There will be arguments, money struggles, and tears. You will face rough seas ahead with family, finances, lifestyles, and everything in between.

Don't be discouraged, something even more wondrous is about to come your way. Comfort. Comfort you have never known was possible and a deep compassionate feeling of being "home." The love you feel right now will grow deeper and higher than you can imagine. You have a partner now and handled correctly, you will have a partner for the rest of your life.

Now that you have promised to love and cherish each other forever, use this wisdom and guidance to make the promises last a lifetime.

Be Realistic!

Now that you have the big dreams, throw in some realism with the rice and bubbles.

The rent/mortgage still needs to be paid. Put one foot in front of the other and be cautiously optimistic with your future goals to avoid discouragement.

Go Big!

You've promised your love and life to him, so why not plan big! Your shared dreams will help keep you together. Express to him your greatest aspirations and encourage him to share his with you. Be his greatest cheerleader. Allow for and encourage change and growth in each other.

Happily Ever After

Set the tone now. If you immediately start mothering him and take care of his every need, he will expect it all the time. After a few months this will become old, and you will resent his inability to take more initiative with the household chores. Show him how you like the clothes folded and the dishwasher loaded. If he doesn't do it to your satisfaction, let it be.

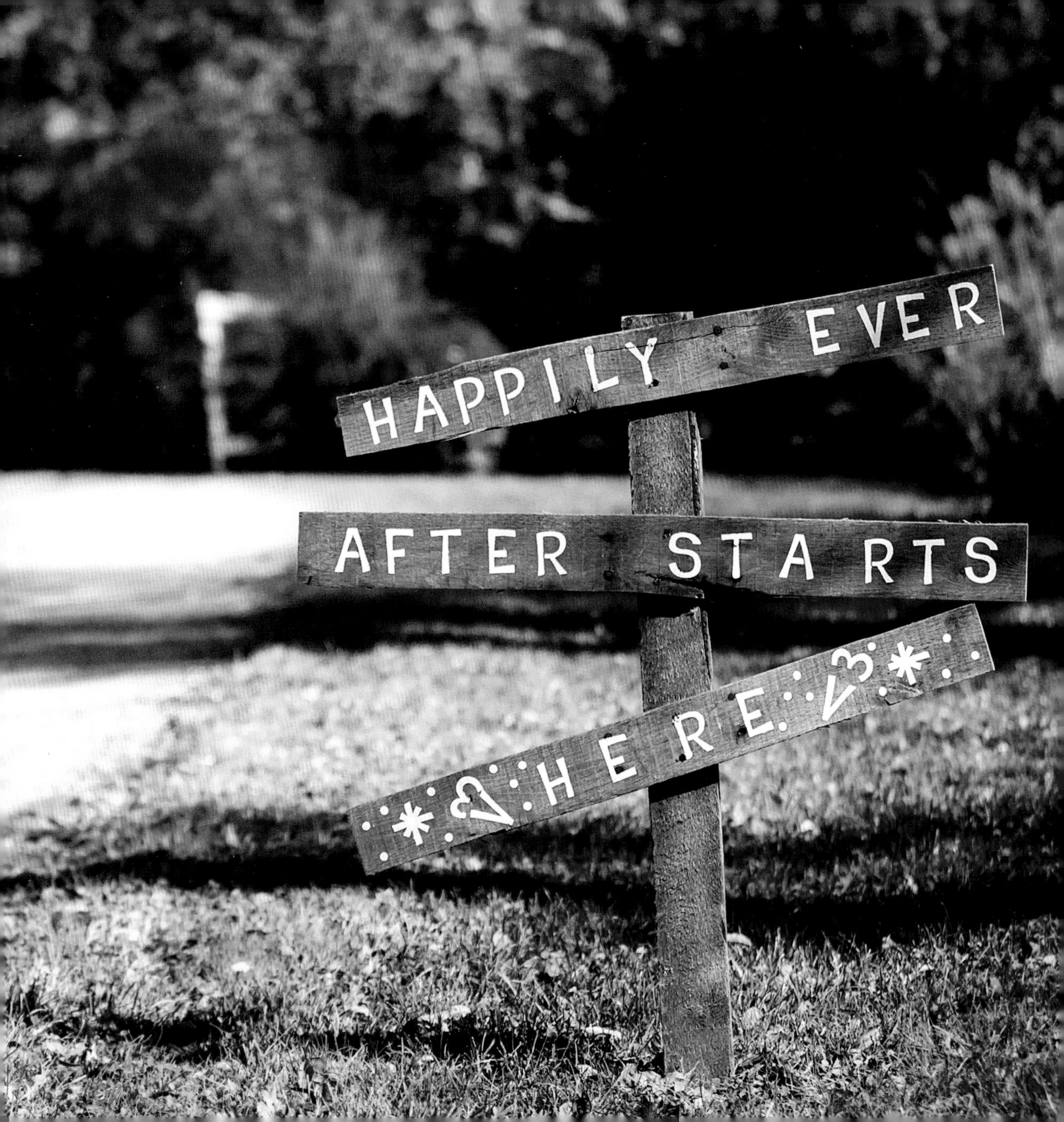
HAPPILY EVER
AFTER STARTS
HERE

Be Apart to Stay Together

Just because you are married does not mean you should abandon your friends and all that existed in your life before your marriage. Outside social activities will bring new life to you and re-energize yourself for your spouse. While it is essential to embrace his desires and needs, don't forget yourself along the way. Over focusing on your relationship may actually harm it. Step away now and then.

The time you spend apart gives you time to decompress, to be yourself, and to secure your identity outside of your marriage. This will also provide you with something new to talk about with your husband.

Build Him Up Buttercup!

There will be times when you have to sacrifice what you want to help the other achieve a goal. It's a game of give and take. Try not to do too much of either.

Complimentary Gift

Over time it becomes easy to take your spouse for granted.
Avoid complacency—show your spouse acknowledgment and
appreciation by recognizing his values in life and in love.
Your husband needs loving affirmation more than you realize.
Women typically receive it from other people while men
seldom show this need.

Cry Baby

You cry and he doesn't. It's OK. Some men just don't show their feelings with tears. We're all different.

What's for Dinner?

If your husband is a reluctant cook, he may be more responsive to being a grill-master.

- Get him a grilling cookbook.
- Buy him a cool apron—be sure to tell him how sexy he looks!

Ebb and Flow

You can't always be on the same wavelength in your marriage. Learn how to ride each other's waves.

Perfect Imperfections

You and your husband each have quirks and annoyances...we all do, that is the reality and beauty of life. Acceptance of each other is of utmost importance. Focus on the positives and let some of those odd habits of his slide by.

Lean on Me

While you spend time together at social events and family functions, this does not count as your "alone" time. Carve out special time to share new experiences and expose each other to what has been happening in your individual lives.

All You Need is Love

We all need love in different and a variety of ways.
Learn the ways your husband needs love.

Not Alone

Never make him feel alone, especially when you are with him.

Rotating Planets

The Venus and Mars analogy is accurate. Men and women are truly different.

The moods of a man are simple and singular. The moods of a woman are vast, extreme, varying, dangerous, and loving.

You will change—often. He might not.

Heart to Heart

Becoming "one" is about more than sex. It requires
a heart to heart vulnerability that opens the door for a
deeper connection.

Listen, Give, Share, Enjoy, Trust, Forgive, and Promise

Do these with total abandon.

Lose an Argument Gracefully

Sometimes it's necessary to give in to your spouse when the argument has reached an impasse. Let no hard feelings linger.

Win an Argument Gracefully

After an argument and you have "won", remember that your husband has probably given in to you out of love.

Little by Little

It is the little things you do which make the difference and fill each other's hearts. It's amazing what a surprise massage will do!

50/50

Nope, marriage is not 50/50—ever. Some days you may have to give your husband 90 percent and he may only give you 10 percent. Other days it will be reversed. Make him aware of the times you need him to pick up the slack.

Accept Your Differences

Be mindful of your emotional baggage and be gentle with your husband's. Just like you, he has strengths and weaknesses.

Celebrate Good Times . . . C'mon!

Are you the type of person who prefers not to make a big deal of your special day or are you of the mindset that your birthday is the one day in the year that everything can and should be about you? Start now and let your husband know which way you believe. Make sure you know how he wants to celebrate his birthday too!

Be Strong

- Do not lose your own identity.

- Do not expect him to meet all your needs.

- Do not let him make all the decisions.

- Avoid being needy and insecure.

- Do not give up your own goals and dreams.

- Do not control him.

- Keep your financial independence.

- Maintain your own friendships.

He's Number One

Your husband is the most important person in your world. You are a team and you must stand by each other. Do not allow friends or family to come between you. Let everyone know you are BFF's.

Hey There Sexy

It's easy and fun to flirt with each other in the beginning of your relationship. Keep the sparks alive by continuing the flirting.

Where Has the Romance Gone?

Life is not a romance novel. Your husband will have smelly socks and various forms of gross behavior. It appears to be in his DNA to have some disgusting habits. Show him the best you can...try to accept the rest.

Pick Your Battles!

Remember these words: Pick your battles! No matter how well-suited you are, it's just not feasible to agree on everything. If you are mature enough to be married, you are mature enough to listen to your spouse. Give a little and teach him (yes, he may need to be taught) how to make compromises.

For Richer or Poorer

Discussions about money are as un-sexy as you can get. However, since this is the number one problem in marriages, start talking about it right away. Managing your own money is a challenge enough. Incorporating your spouse's finances can be overwhelming. The two of you need to take time to discuss how you would like to handle your finances.

- Design a budget.

- Build an estate plan.

- Max out your retirement plans.

- Have an emergency account.

- Get out of debt and stay out of debt.

- Save no less than 10% of your gross salaries.

He Said/She Said

The number one rule for a successful marriage is communication. It is also number two, number three, and every other number! Never stop getting to know your spouse. Talk about politics, music, food, and everything and anything that is important in your life. When you are comfortable having everyday conversations, you will find it easier to guide through more difficult topics.

Talk about everything, talk about anything.

Fine! Nothing is Wrong! Whatever!

Avoid these words. Tell him what you are feeling and what you need from him. He is not a mind-reader. Perfect guys do not exist but remember he's the one you chose.

Mommy!

It will be easy to run to your Mom or friends for advice and comfort when your spouse does something you don't like. Stop yourself! While having a close confidant to vent to may help you keep sane, respect the privacy of your marriage.

Love Notes

- Tell him he's handsome and desirable.
- Take a class together.
- Text him to let him know you are thinking of him.
- Always kiss goodnight.
- Hold hands.
- Leave love notes.
- Dance.
- Start traditions.
- Say thank you.
- Put down the electronics.
- Be kind...always.
- Never blame, criticize or say things you know will hurt.
- Be mindful of your emotional baggage and be gentle with his.
- Plan your future together.
- Make time for sex.

Get ready for the ride of your life! Being married will bring you happiness, hardship, great heights, and difficult lows. It won't always be easy and it won't always be fun. Shoulder the difficult times and rejoice in the delights together. Keep your mutual love as a center point in your life, and it will be more than worth it.

Best wishes for a joyous journey!

Dear Bride
Advice for the Newlywed

Written by Judy Smith
Design by Magdalena Snowman

Published by Holland Publishing
130 Thornhill Ln, Newtown, PA 18940
www.hollandpublishinggroup.com

ISBN: 978-0-9961415-3-6
Library of Congress Control Number:

Book and jacket design:
Magdalena Snowman

Printed in Malaysia